Patterns of perception

by

Ken W Simpson

Augur Press

PATTERNS OF PERCEPTION

Copyright © Ken W Simpson 2015

The moral right of the author has been asserted

British Library Cataloguing in Publication Data.
A catalogue record for this book is available from
the British Library.

ISBN 978-0-9571380-7-0

First published 2015 by
Augur Press
Delf House
52 Penicuik Road
Roslin
Midlothian EH25 9LH
United Kingdom

Printed by Lightning Source

Patterns of perception

Dedication

To my daughter, Tuan Tran Lee, her husband Minh, my niece Carole and to my 'muse', Jodie Kewley.

Contents

Preface

Introduction

Preface

Ken was reared in a family that was unable to give him a sense of meaning and connection with life – something that he wanted and needed. The last two poems in this collection – *Cold Turkey* and *Indifference* – convey that situation very clearly.

His early years channelled him into becoming a 'detached' observer of life. And yet his poems carry in them evidence of passionate involvement, albeit masked. That he achieves this expression poetically and without any use of rhyme is intriguing.

His own comment on rhyme is as follows:

Byronic

The romantic legacy
of yesterday
rhyme
at the end of lines
continues
to contaminate
contemporary poetry

Although eloquently put, this is part of the mask. The real reason for the absence of rhyme bites much deeper and forms an essential part of the potency of his expression.

Another very relevant aspect is that Ken is a trained artist. His artistic talents come together with his poetic expression to create pictures in the mind. These pictures move and flow. They are multidimensional, communicating deeper messages than the words might at first appear to convey.

Introduction

I was born at South Camberwell, a suburb of Melbourne, just before WW2. I was the first of a family of three boys.

After primary school I was enrolled at Scotch College, where I spent several fruitless years until the age of fifteen. After that I worked for my father, a chartered accountant, as an audit clerk. Numbers meant very little to me, but I stuck it out for three years. Then I worked as a despatch clerk at a furniture store for another three years.

My father noticed my artistic bent and spoke to his cousin who taught graphic art. This resulted in my taking a drawing test at Swinburne College and being accepted for a four-year diploma course there.

The course was academic and 'old school'. The first two years (the Certificate of art) were spent learning to draw accurately from life and casts. There were also design-related subjects - including pottery. I chose to specialise in painting for the final two years. This was academically oriented - with still life and portrait painting in oils, and drawing with charcoal, chalk and pastels. We also studied the history of art, and had to matriculate in English expression.

I worked as an art teacher in technical schools for the next fifteen years, broken only by a trip to the UK in 1958.

I was superannuated due to stress-related illness towards the end of the 1960s. I had already written a short story, which had been valued by an English teacher. Now, in a new phase of my life, I wrote more.

It was about ten years ago when I first began to write poetry. I soon discovered that free verse was a natural mode of expression for me.

I have had seven poetry books published by SBPRA and Sanbun, a small press in New Delhi. Ideas occur to me almost every day, and I continue to distil the essence of these into new poems.

I have a rich family life as I live with my daughter, her husband and their four children at Lysterfield in Victoria, Australia.

POEMS

Pollution

Imitation clouds
flakes of yellow ochre
in a china-white sky
detached for a moment
from a molten mountain
bordered in black
where minds
paralysed by greed reside
left behind
as an abstraction
in a jungle of indifference.

Born to Die Again

The avenue to paradise
I was told
is up the stairs
and to the right
past the remains of yesterday
prominently displayed
amidst the ruins of tomorrow.

Insight

A gleam of light
intrudes inside a room
defining dust particles
glowing motes, and eyes
wandering, wondering
obliquely watching.

Compatibility

The truth lives alone
existing wherever you go
inside or outside.

Cheers

Illusions of truth
distilled or fermented
as wine and spirits.

Credo

Limited propriety
seems to be the epitome
of opportunism and greed.

Nightmare

The moods of a lifetime
condensed, revived
to haunt the night.

Tints of Gold

Blushing, fading
descending
fragile autumn leaves
blending
with each passing moment.

Watercolour Words

Distant forests
seem to levitate
through wispy mists
with fluttering leaves
disconcerted
by a teasing breeze
with ancient trees
that benignly sway
towards rippling reflections
dancing with water-lilies.

An Elegy

The tear gleamed
and slid
slowly down her cheek
as a vision
reflecting her face
beautiful and stricken
delicately poised
timelessly frozen
like a diamond
immortalised
in a moment of grief.

Baloney

Gushing words
overflow
from an artificial mouth
attached to a microphone
in a crowded hall.

Booming sounds merge
and resonate as lies
disguised as promises
that echo
around each wall.

Consanguinity

Life's apotheosis
is something in between
a state of decay
a compost heap
a sprouting seed
and creativity
using thoughts and ideas
to express individuality.

The link between
fantasy and reality
creates sense
out of nonsense
by contemplating
meditating, inventing
and eventually disintegrating.

Curiosity

Tell me
why melancholy
infects your mind
while waiting
for the tide to ebb
and reveal the detritus
or revelations
you should have known
years ago.

Tokens

Interpretations
of scattered moments
are lost in time.

Fragments
of unspoken thoughts
disappear with the wind.

Declamations die
like drops of rain
never to be heard again.

Anecdotes roam
like ghosts
all over the countryside.

An Autumn Interlude

Basking in the afternoon sun
glittering through a gap
between languid clouds
drifting in a solemn sky
above
some neglected pelargoniums
flowering somehow
bordered by a patch of grass
where Turtle Doves
industriously flutter
peck then begin to fade
as my eyelids droop
losing focus
until revived
by the coolness
of a passing breeze.

Contented Breezes

A glorious summer dawning
over the awakening bay
serene blue wavelets
rolling, foaming
a canoe slides by
speeding launches
head out to sea
the sky peers down
through wispy clouds
wafted by a caressing breeze
a tanned lady
strides resolutely by
her long dark hair flying
behind a determined face
preceded by a Labrador
regally trotting
swooping gulls excitedly scream
between sea and sky.

The Morning Sting

One dull summer Sunday morning
I went swimming in the bay
on my back out to sea
gazing upwards at shredded clouds
like cotton wool
broken by jagged rents
peeping through
of white, brilliant sunlight.

I passed a yellow buoy
bumped into something lumpy
just beneath the surface
changed course
and began swimming back to shore
in a choppy swell
when stung
by a giant jelly-fish.

Programmed

The mind
aged around twenty-three
is purportedly free
and qualified to choose
a fulfilling career
by successfully applying
for a job
as a wage earner
to commute
and predictably marry
arrange a loan for a home
routinely raise a family
responsibly, respectably
patriotically
every dogmatic, manipulated day.

Room for Regret

Plastic flowers
on a mantelpiece
with ivory elephants
where a clock chimed
each quarter hour
of a best forgotten time
where ageing memories
of children playing
are revived
in fading pictures
on an angry wall
boxed in by banalities
and routine activities
distracted by voices
that echo inside
the mausoleum of the mind
while yesterday lingers
like an unwelcome guest
where only
the plastic flowers are fresh.

The Reality of a Dream

I slept and dreamed
an actor
forced to play a role
in every scene.

I had friends
who were strangers
so set off alone
uncertain where to go.

I remembered a hut
on a cliff-top
which existed
only in my mind.

I tried to cross a lake
but it merged
into a maze of streets
where I lost my way.

Unable to afford a ticket
I boarded a train
but soon realised
it was going the wrong way.

Rural View

Frogs croaked
from watery ditches
beside a lazy lane
and cows placidly grazed
in paddocks
beneath a fading sky
tinted pink.

Aristocratic crows
snubbed
a cabaret of sparrows
performing
beside an arthritic tree
sparsely draped
with a mantle of leaves.

Lengthening shadows
from the departing sun
spread across
the pastel land
in a rich tapestry
of hues
mauve, red and gold.

Air Conditioning

A cobalt sky
fading to white
glows benignly
in the morning light.

Leafy canopies
listlessly hang
on a lonely tree
inside a nature strip.

Untidy shrubs
confined behind a hedge
fail to conceal
screaming graffiti on a wall.

Traffic builds
on grim, grey bitumen
groaning
like a beast in agony.

Curtains
and artificial air
replace the sky
with TV images and insecticide.

Touring Blues

Absorb the grandeur
of historical places
where worn cobblestones
unevenly spaced
torment tourists' feet
tottering
past souvenir shops
to photograph the scenery.

Coaches congregate
identical shells
inanimate, empty
until tourists
board
then come to life
accelerate
as motor ignites
and gears change.

Camera buffs
obsessively snap
gargoyles and gables
risking decapitation
when floating beneath bridges
or rising in a bouncing cart
to record
the rear end of a horse.

Early in the morning
indistinguishable coaches
hit the highways
with cargoes of clones
force-fed facts
unrelentingly
until lethargy and apathy
take their toll.

Words of Infatuation

Her hair glows
like a raven's wing
framing an oval face
above
a gorgeous form
soft and slender hands
lovely calves
and exquisite feet.

Carved from Clouds

Liz
fleetingly glimpsed
ethereal, alone
between shades of blue
the sky and lake
canopies of sheltering trees
song birds
and a mountain stream
where the image of her smiling face
reappears inside my mind
as true as love and memory
can ever be.

Looking Back

Thoughts escape
as silent echoes
memories
of wistful yearnings
for soft, warm hands
and a slender waist.

A fragile love
that failed to last
but reappears sometimes
in blissful dreams
as fantasies
or variations on a theme.

Greetings

As I strolled casually by
I heard a low, sweet voice
and saw a smile
so tender and charming.

I smiled shyly back
and exchanged a few words
as I thought
a deposit on the future.

She accompanied me
like blissful music
that matched the euphoria
inside my mind.

Terrestrial
and botanical delights
enveloped me
in their warm embrace.

Our meal that night
was an epicurean delight
to savour
taste and masticate.

Her image
was locked within my mind
yet separated
by cruel reality.

Although apart
we kept in touch
like phantoms
on the internet.

I carried her with me
everywhere
like a talisman
or puppet on a string.

Mortally beautiful
a wreath of flowers
crowned her brow
like a halo.

With skin like silk
and jet black hair
she lay motionless
cold as marble.

Familiarity

Our first home
a depression-style bungalow
was like the others
with roses in front
and a vine behind.

I remember
my mother's violin
which she couldn't play
a relic
from her school days.

She didn't read
but loved
to socialise
screaming with laughter
when playing cards.

I had two brothers
like strangers
and a gay uncle
with a partner
who laughed like a hyena.

On weekends
we'd visit
our grandparents
swim, sunbathe
and search for crabs.

Dolly

Aged five or six
a city child
I was driven
to the countryside
for a holiday
on a dairy farm.

Looking back
at bits and pieces
of faded images
blurred and indistinct
like squashed insects
on a windscreen.

Flattened paddocks
rushing by
pale diffused washes
of warm evening colours
satiated
by the summer heat.

My father left behind
squawking fowls
pecking industriously
some quacking ducks
and exotic
farmyard smells.

I hunted for eggs
amidst heaps of straw
and crossed a log bridge
over a creek
where shy, wild turkeys
sometimes hid.

We bounced over paddocks
in an ancient car
stopping
while the radiator cooled
and eventually arrived
at a picnic site.

In the yard one day
Mr Mason
the farmer
invited me to ride
a huge draught horse
but I timorously declined.

I was fed
vast quantities
of cauliflower
a tasteless vegetable
in the kitchen
at each monotonous meal.

A pony patiently waited
while a farmhand
hoisted me into the saddle
and adjusted the stirrups
while I sat like a king
blissfully happy.

She knew where to go
leisurely plodding
towards a paddock
where cows were moving
through a gap
towards the milking shed.

We ambled along a dirt track
on our last ride together
to meet a distant vehicle
spewing clouds of dust
driven by my father
to return me to the city.

Cold Turkey

One winter
I was sent to stay
with my grandpa
who played bowls
and my grandma
who didn't care.

An interloper
I was left alone
to wander
the cliff tops
frowned upon
by towering pines.

Grey wavelets
slopped
against enigmatic rocks
and a fishing boat
dipped laboriously
in the swell.

I trod
the slippery boards
of a distended pier
as waves sprayed
slapping against
calloused piles.

Charcoal clouds
in the sky
moped
above me
melancholy
in their indifference.

Indifference

Gradations of grey
and shadows
stretch into twilight
when darkness intervenes.

The mind matures
like grapes
manipulated and squeezed
to bleed internally.

Silent evocations
come to mind
of parental indifference
and brotherly animosity.

My father
a stranger to me
laughed uproariously
at Charlie Chaplin.

Obscure days
of Sunday ways
tacitly prejudiced
and pretentiously pious.

My lunch inside
a brown-paper bag
creamed-honey sandwiches
and a hard-boiled egg.

Then the desolation
of adolescence
carnally captured
shamed and enraptured.

The conformity
of respectability
induced a wistful yearning
to be disrespectful.

For other titles from Augur Press
please visit

www.augurpress.com

www.ingramcontent.com/pod-product-compliance
Lightning Source LLC
LaVergne TN
LVHW041238080426
835508LV00011B/1274